Dude, Seriously! 41 Ways You Are Sabotaging Your Sales Career and How to Fix Them Before You Go Broke!

From Tim

I would like to dedicate this book to my wife Angie, who has stayed on my butt to get it done! And to all those people along the way who refused to let me slack off!

From Nick

I would like to dedicate this book to my parents Bill and Celeste Thomas for their neverending encouragement and support. Their inspiration gave me the strength and dedication to get me through many of life's valleys.

Contents

Tim and Nick's Top Ten Commandments
for a Successful Career in Sales _____ 5

Preface _____ 6

Your Thinking is All Jacked Up! _____ 8

You Have More Excuses Than Sales! _____ 10

You Think Everyone is Your Customer! _____ 12

You Have a Really Crappy Work Ethic! _____ 14

You Do Not Have a Plan! _____ 16

You Do Not Follow Up! _____ 18

You Do Not Carry Business Cards
With You All the Time! _____ 20

You Do Not Keep a Database, nor Do You
Keep In Touch with Your Clients! _____ 22

At Some Point You Have to Stop Thinking
and Get Off Your Butt and Start Doing! _____ 24

You Do Not Invest In Yourself! _____ 26

You Do Not Work In Your Strength Zone! _____ 28

You Do Not Set Goals! _____ 30

You Do Not Track Your Goals! _____ 32

You Expect People to Buy From You, But
You Dress Like Your Homeless! _____ 34

You Never Take Action! _____ 36

You Are Ashamed of What You Sell
and Don't Even Use it Yourself! _____ 38

You Do Not Plan for the Future! _____ 40

You Do Not Ask for Referrals! _____ 42

You Think that Your Company Owes You Something! _____ 44

You Are Chronically Late for Appointments! _____ 46

You Do Not Return Calls Promptly! _____ 48

You Do Not Have a Clear Sales Presentation and Worse Yet You Are Unprepared! _____ 50

You Never Read Any Books! _____ 52

You Think You Know it All! _____ 54

You Think Networking Groups Are a Waste of Time! _____ 56

You Take Sales Advice From Broke Sales People! _____ 58

You Complain All the Time! _____ 60

You Show Up Late and Leave Early! _____ 62

You See People as Dollar Signs and Not Life Time Relationships! _____ 64

You Do Not Take Care of Your Health! _____ 66

You Do Not Control You're your Thoughts and Emotions! _____ 68

You Strive for Mediocrity! _____ 70

You Do Not Try New Things! _____ 72

You Think Facebook is A Fad! _____ 74

You Hate Change! _____ 76

You Have No Passion! _____ 78

You Do Not Know Your Product! _____ 80

You Do Not Listen to Your Customers! _____ 82

You Do Not Ask for the Business! _____ 84

You Have a Fear of Failure! _____ 87

You Have a Fear of Success! _____ 89

Tim and Nick's Top Ten Commandments for a Successful Career in Sales

1. Have fun & be passionate about your life!
2. Be focused and committed to excellence!
3. Tell the truth!
4. Own your mistakes!
5. Under promise and over deliver!
6. Be a friend first!
7. Have a strong work ethic and make a sale a day!
8. Have a great attitude!
9. Have confidence and follow up!
10. Above all know that you and only you are responsible for your life, your actions, and your career!

Preface

Someone asked us, "Why are you going to write this book?" And that is a great question! We wrote this book to help sales people everywhere really understand what it takes to make it in the world of selling. Too many people fail, not because of a lack of talent, but really because of a lack of discipline.

You must have drive, determination, passion, and daily disciplines to be successful in every area of your life-**but you really need these in sales!**

And here is why...

Because if you do not make sales (that means money), then you don't have a job or a business, you only have an expensive hobby!

And here is another fact...

All the knowledge in this book is not going to make you one sale, because reading it is not enough. You must take the knowledge we are sharing with you and actually apply it in your business. You have to take action!

We have made it really simple to take action because we have provided you with action items in each chapter. Now we are not going to guarantee that if you do these items you will explode your sales because you may not even need to be in sales in the first place.

The business of sales is not for everyone! You need to know up front that if you are not cut out for selling, then for Heaven's sake find a new career! Stop beating your head against the wall and frustrating everyone around you by continuing to make it in a career that you suck at!

The root of selling is people. You need to like people. You need to like to be around people, talk to them, find out their problems, and ask them for the business. If you read that and think…"man that is not me!" then that is your clue to find another career!

Now we say this in love because there is nothing worse than a friend who will not tell you the truth just to spare your feelings. That is not really a friend.

We have been in the world of sales our entire working career. We have sold everything from toothbrushes to toilet brushes and during the journey we have uncovered the 41 Ways You Are Sabotaging Your Sales Career and How to Fix Them Before You Go Broke.

Here is another cold, hard, and brutal truth…

Your sales are not in the toilet because of the economy or any other excuse…they are in the toilet because of you. If you want better results change what you are doing! If not, then keep doing what you have been and you will watch your bank account dry up.

Hopefully you have figured it out by now that this is not a Dr. Phil make you feel better, warm and fuzzy book. We tried that and it didn't work too well. This is an in your face, what we do to make money, sales book. Everything we will teach you is what we do everyday to keep business rolling in the door. Some of it is easy, some of it is hard, but all of it is necessary to selling.

Another thing about this book is that it is not long. Neither one of us are big fans of reading. We read because it is necessary. We figured that most of you were like us and didn't want to read another 500 page book on sales, so we made this short, sweet, and to the point. Plus both of us are more talkers than writer's anyhow so short is better for us as well. We think this is a win-win.

So how about we stop with the small talk and get on with how to fix your sales before you go broke and have to ask us for a draw against commissions…

Your Thinking is All Jacked Up!

Tim and Nick's Famous Quote Validation!

(Because we figure that if you don't believe us, then maybe you will believe a famous quote for goodness sake!)

"Change Your Thoughts and You Change Your World"

– Norman Vincent Peale

Every wrong action begins first as a thought. If you need to change your actions. you must change your thinking! If you don't think anyone will not buy your product or service, then you are right – they won't!! Your mind is powerful beyond measure. It will throw self defeating thoughts at you faster than a Nolan Ryan curve ball. You must win the battle in your mind. It is a constant fight that you must win every day, if you are going to win in sales.

Your brain and mind is, without a doubt, the most sophisticated computer in the universe. Zig Ziglar said that if you took all of the computers in the world and all of their power, then combined them into one super computer they could still not do the one thing your mind can do in a split second. That one thing is-**create a thought!** We want you to think about that for a moment.

You can instantly create a thought! The power is that **YOU** have control over the thoughts you create. You can choose to create positive and energetic thoughts, or you can sit around a dwell on why everyone else wins, but you. The choice is yours.

There is one very simple thought that can destroy your day, your month, and your life. That one simple thought is doubt. Everyone deals with doubt and no one is exempt from doubt trying to enter the mind. The difference is simply that some people choose to let doubt move in, set up residence, and stay forever and other people kick doubt to the curb! The choice is yours!

Everyday you must realize that the battle to win is the battle in your mind. You must, **on purpose**, set out to win this battle at all cost. We are going to challenge you throughout this book and we guarantee that doubt is going to try and get in. The question is…will you let it stay?

You Have More Excuses Than Sales!

> Tim and Nick's Famous Quote Validation!
> (Because we figure that if you don't believe us, maybe you will believe a famous quote for goodness sake!)
>
> **"99% of all failure comes from people who have a habit of making excuses!"**
> –George Washington Carver

Dude, Seriously…how many excuses are you going to come up with to justify your lack of sales? The real truth is that no one wants to hear your excuses anyway. Here are our top 10 excuses and answers to help you look beyond your circumstance.

1. The economy is bad – **Make more sales calls and change your mind.**
2. We don't have training – **educate yourself.**
3. My computer isn't working – **it doesn't make sales either, so get a pen and paper and start writing orders.**
4. I am tired – **get more sleep, try going to bed earlier.**
5. No one is buying – **you are right! The two people you talked to said no, find some more.**
6. It is really tough out there – **yep it is! You have to fight through it!**
7. I can't get past the gatekeeper – **develop a relationship with them, they are people too!**
8. The media is telling my client not to buy – **overcome the media with the real facts!**
9. Our price too high – **it always will be, that is how you get paid! Stop focusing on price!**
10. I don't have the right business cards, letterhead, or sales flyer – **so what, sell anyway!**

We know you have more than these, but quite frankly carpel tunnel syndrome will set in if we type them all out. Excuses are developed in your mind. You must stop letting these thoughts develop and the only way to crowd them out is to fill up on sales, marketing, and motivation!

You Think Everyone is Your Customer!

Tim and Nick's Famous Quote Validation!
(Because we figure that if you don't believe us, maybe you will believe a famous quote for goodness sake!)

"The secret to being the best in the world is to make the world smaller!"
–Seth Godin

We may beat our brains in trying to get this point across, but it will be well worth it! You have customers right now that you wish would lose your phone number and at the same time you are to scared to let them go. You will let them beat you up on price, wear you out with request, and call you at all hours, just so that you don't lose that commission check.

This is a sure recipe for disaster. At some point you are going to break. You are running around like a chicken with your head cut off trying to satisfy someone you really don't like, just to earn a pay check. And we have heard all the excuses on this as well! Someone once said, "But if I do a good job for them, they will send me referrals!"

That is true, but likes hang around likes, and there is a really good chance that their friends are going to be just like them! If that is what you really want, then have at it, but these are the people that cause your sales to suck.

You will always get 80% of your business from the top 20% of your customers. You need to be on the hunt for more of these people. You need to narrow your target to a specific niche. The narrower and the more focused the more time and money you will make. It is just a plain fact!

Here is exactly what you need to do in order to bring some sanity and fun to your career!

1. Identify your favorite clients! Who are they? What do they do? Why do they buy from you? (and it won't be because of price!)

2. Develop a strategy to get in front of more of these people! Join their organizations, affiliate with their circles of influence, and develop a message to attract them to you!

3. Create a following! Attract these people to you through your marketing. Focus on being their problem solver! (Solving problems is where you get paid big bucks! The bigger the problem, the more they pay and the less they shop!)

You Have a Really Crappy Work Ethic!

Tim and Nick's Famous Quote Validation!

(Because we figure that if you don't believe us, maybe you will believe a famous quote for goodness sake!)

"Far and away the best prize that life has to offer is the chance to work hard at work worth doing!"

–Theodore Roosevelt

You probably are already aware of this, but just to be on the safe side, we want to make sure that you understand that what you put it, will always equal what you get out!

The biggest reason people say that they are attracted to sales, is the freedom and flexibility it provides. This is also the biggest reason for failure! Flexibility to pick your kids up from school is awesome, but when you let that flexibility creep into other parts of the day, then you are in for a rude awakening!

One of the biggest trends these days is work from home. Many companies are embracing this culture but if you are one of those people who have a home office, then you need to make sure that you treat it the same way you would if you were going to an office.

This means you have to get up, get dressed, and have set work hours! You do not get to go to the kitchen and watch Oprah. In fact, if you are in sales, then you need to leave the house during the day and go see clients!

We have found that even though people desire the flexibility, they also need a schedule to keep them moving in the right direction. Here is a simple schedule for you to start following each day!

- ✓ 5-7 AM Get Up. Get Dressed. Get Moving!
- ✓ 8-8:30 AM Read email, send out 5 cards
- ✓ 8:30-10AM Prospect for new clients
- ✓ 10 – 11AM Return morning phone calls
- ✓ 11 – 12 Lunch (with a client or referral partner)
- ✓ 12 – 2 PM Prospect for new business
- ✓ 2 – 3 PM Return Afternoon calls
- ✓ 3 – 5 Prospect some more!
- ✓ 5 – 5:30 PM Set your schedule for the next day!
- ✓ Repeat!

You Do Not Have a Plan!

Tim and Nick's Famous Quote Validation!

(Because we figure that if you don't believe us, maybe you will believe a famous quote for goodness sake!)

"First comes thought; then organization of that thought, into ideas and plans; then transformation of those plans into reality"

–Napoleon Hill

Dude, Seriously…how many times have you been told that you need a plan to succeed? Have you ever heard the statement…"*if you fail to plan, then you plan to fail?*" We see this **ALL** the time in business and sales. So why is it that so many sales people never take the time to write out a plan? Here is what we have come up with to answer that question…

1. They do not know how
2. They think it is complicated
3. They are lazy

Now you get to choose which one of these statements represents you! The first two we can fix, but the third is something you must fix if you want to be successful. Putting together a plan is simple, but you must know your numbers, so to make it easy we have put together a simple form that you will get at the end of the book!

What you need to do today put together a plan. It doesn't have to be long, complicated, or have 700 steps, but it does need to be simple and something that you will fully commit to doing. We know a lot of people with plans and all they do is shove them in a desk drawer somewhere, never review them and ultimately forget about them!.

One simple strategy that is an absolute must to your plan is to make at least one sale per day. In fact, as you work out your plan, every activity you do, should be leading to the result of you making a sale. Why go to a networking meeting if you are not expecting for that to lead to a sale? Why send letters, e-mails, or cards if you do not expect them to lead to a sale? Everything you do must be designed with the intent to lead to a sale.

It has to be a driving instinct in your gut that when you wake up, get up, and go out that your sole mission that day is to make a sale. It doesn't guarantee your success but it will help you line up your activities instead of roaming around aimlessly like a lost puppy dog. Write down a long term plan, a short term plan, and a DAILY plan! Be intentional about your day, career, and life!

You Do Not Follow Up!

Tim and Nick's Famous Quote Validation!

(Because we figure that if you don't believe us, maybe you will believe a famous quote for goodness sake!)

"You have to have confidence in your ability, and then be tough enough to follow through."

-Rosalynn Carter

Dude, Seriously… how many leads did you get in the last month that you have not followed up with until they either said yes or leave me the heck alone? Just because a prospect says no to your first offer, doesn't mean that they will always say no. In fact, it has been proven that it take somewhere between 5-7 follow up contacts before the average sale is made. If you are like most sales people, they get told no and here is what happens next…

- **They become discouraged**
- **They pout and cry**
- **They don't get the prospects information to follow up**
- **They think the prospect rejected THEM and not the offer**
- **They call it day and say something like…"that is just the sales game…"**

All of these are self-sabotaging! Stop it now! Sale's is all about the follow up. Just because they don't buy today, doesn't mean they won't by next week, next month, or next year! If you want to win in the game of sales, you need to practice the **PPPITB Principle**. You need to make sure you are a **Professionally Persistent Pain in the Butt** Until They Buy. One of the very best things you can do to correct this today is every time you meet with a prospect, make sure you do these 4 things…

1. **Send them a personal thank you card**
2. **Follow up with a phone call and ask for referrals**
3. **Send them regular emails and cards.**
4. **Repeat until they buy, refer you, or tell you to leave them the heck alone.**

If you need a system to help you do this, then check out www.maximumsalesgenerator.com

You Do Not Carry Business Cards With You All the Time!

Tim and Nick's Famous Quote Validation!

(Because we figure that if you don't believe us, maybe you will believe a famous quote for goodness sake!)

"I say luck is when opportunity comes along and you are prepared for it!"

–Denzel Washington

Dude, Seriously…a business card is the most basic, simple, and fundamental tool you have in sales. You should ALWAYS have business cards with you, because you never know when you are going to run into someone who needs your product or service.

Sure there are obvious places to carry your business cards, like a networking event, but you would be surprised at how many people over the years have told me excuses like these…

- I forgot my cards
- They are at the printer
- I ran out (Seriously???)

Blah, blah, blah…get your cards and keep them with you at all times! Here are some places to put your cards at today…

- ✓ Your wallet or purse. Some of you need to even put them in your wife's purse.
- ✓ Your car and your spouse's car.
- ✓ Your suit coats or jacket pockets.
- ✓ Your computer case or briefcase.
- ✓ Your Male European Carry-All, or "murse" (That is a male purse)

You need to be passing out cards like it was Halloween and everyone is coming to your house! And while you are at it, maybe you should be collecting business cards as well. Do not make the fatal mistake that if you hand out cards that people will be beating down your door and burning up the phone to buy from you…heck no! You have to collect cards, put them in your database, follow up with people and then ask for the business!

Now don't go freaking out on us. We cover how to do all of these in this book, just keep reading.

You Do Not Keep a Database, nor Do You Keep In Touch with Your Clients!

Tim and Nick's Famous Quote Validation!

(Because we figure that if you don't believe us, maybe you will believe a famous quote for goodness sake!)

"Treasure your relationships, not your possessions!"
–Anthony J. D'Angelo

Dude, Seriously…one main reason you keep working hard, running fast, and beating your head against a wall looking for new clients is because you have failed to keep a database of all of your prospects, and closed clients. Seriously, who is more likely to refer you and do business with you again than a happy client? We have given this advice to business owners and sales people our entire career, but few of them actually implement this simple strategy. It usually starts out with questions like…

- **What type of database is the best?**
    - Answer: The one you will actually use!
- **How often should I send something and call them?**
    - Answer: 8-12 times per year
- **What should I send them?**
    - Answer: Company news, promotions, and offers. You should even send them Birthday Cards!! We have built every business we have off of birthday cards, because people never care how much you know, until they know how much you care!
- **Who do I put in my database?**
    - Answer: Everyone! Past clients, prospects, neighbors and even the pizza guy! Why? Because you never know who someone knows! The best database will allow you to group people into categories. This way you can better target your message for optimal results!

Do not over think this strategy (in fact we have a chapter in this book about not over thinking! Maybe you should go and read that chapter now!). You just simply need to do it. In fact we have made it real simple to get started with your very own database! Check out this site and get started today! www.maximumsalesgenerator.com

At Some Point You Have to Stop Thinking and Get Off Your Butt and Start Doing!

Tim and Nick's Famous Quote Validation!

(Because we figure that if you don't believe us, maybe you will believe a famous quote for goodness sake!)

"Procrastination is the grave in which opportunity is buried!" –

Author Unknown

(sorry, but we included this one because, well it is GOOD!)

Sorry to let you down, but business will never be perfect. Where do you think Bill Gates would be today if he never started and just kept thinking about building computers? For that matter, we would be pecking this book out on a typewriter, and going thru massive amounts of white out! Thank God, he took action!

We tell people all the time that he became ridiculously rich because he would put out a product, the consumer would tell him what they would like to see or have in the next versions and BAM…he would create version 2.0, then version 3.0, and so on. Not a bad plan if you ask us!

Business and sales are dynamic, because customers are demanding. They always want something new, bigger, and better. By the time some of you actually get around to taking action on an idea, the consumer has already moved on. We see people all the time that go to sales conferences and get all jacked up on the speaker's presentations, but they NEVER implement any of the ideas! They over think everything!

So let us say it one more time…just do it already! It will never be perfect, but that is the magic. Let your clients tell you how to make it better, then improve on your product or service. This is actually one of the best kept marketing secrets in business today! The movers, shakers, and money makers know that taking action quickly, results in constantly having to order check deposit slips…not a bad thing when you are in business!

- **What idea do you have right now that you have yet to implement?**
- **What is the next step you need to take to make it happen?**
- **When will you do this buy? (It is critical to set a deadline!)**
- **Who can you tell that will hold you accountable?**

You Do Not Invest In Yourself!

Tim and Nick's Famous Quote Validation!
(Because we figure that if you don't believe us, maybe you will believe a famous quote for goodness sake!)

"An investment in knowledge always pays the best interest!"
–Benjamin Franklin

Zig Ziglar was once told that "motivational messages are great, but motivation just doesn't last" to which he responded…"that is right, motivation doesn't last, and neither does bathing, that is why I recommend you do both daily!"

Years ago we were at a sales meeting and we were asking a local account rep who was the best sales person in town. She gave me his name and I asked her why this person was so good? You know what she said? She told me that his car was full of sales and motivation CD's. She told us that if anyone rode in his car they could expect to listen to great information from sales coaches, motivational speakers, pastors, and anyone who had a message that he could learn and grow from!

Amazing! This person understood the value of feeding the mind constantly! Your mind is going to try its best to trick you, deceive you, and place doubt in you. You must battle this at every angle! Investing in yourself is by far the best investment you will ever make! Money will come and go, but the investment you make in yourself will last a lifetime!

Did you know that listening to sales training and motivational messages in you car during your normal drive time over the course of one year is the equivalent of getting a four year degree at an accredited college!!! Now that you know, if you continue to not invest in yourself then quit complaining about how bad your sales are.

Here is our quick checklist to help get you pointed in the right direction…

- **How many sales and motivation audios do you own?**
- **How many do you listen too?**
- **When was the last time you went to a seminar?**

You Do Not Work In Your Strength Zone!

Tim and Nick's Famous Quote Validation!

(Because we figure that if you don't believe us, maybe you will believe a famous quote for goodness sake!)

"Use what talents you possess: the woods would be very silent if no birds sang except those that sang the very best!"

–Henry Van Dyke

Dude, Seriously! The reason they call it your "Strength" or your Core Competencies, is because you're good in this area. The opposite is also true; you are not good in your weakness. In business we call this Inefficiency.

We don't know if you've realized this but, inefficient businesses do not succeed (inefficient is a fancy term for not making a lot of money). So dude, seriously, if you are not operating in your strength then by default you are probably experiencing high blood pressure, lack of money and a huge mountain you can't seem to overcome. These are all side effects of working in your weakness.

Save yourself a tremendous amount of time and headaches and get your tail in the line of work that comes natural to you. Here you will find success, peace of mind and fulfillment. We recommend a personality profile to point out what your strengths and weaknesses- go to www.themarketingevangelist.com/strengthfinder

Once you know the areas you are best in, you can outsource task that you are not good at doing. If you are great at meeting people, but stink at paperwork, then find an assistant who is really great with details! The money you invest in an assistant, will more than pay for itself in the number of sales you will be able to make.

Side effects of working in your weaknesses:
- Extreme frustration/anxiety
- Lack of Passion/Fulfillment
- Lack of Success
- Experiencing time management issues

Results of Working in your strength:
- Better time management
- Greater opportunity for success
- A healthy drive and passion for what you do

You Do Not Set Goals!

Tim and Nick's Famous Quote Validation!

(Because we figure that if you don't believe us, maybe you will believe a famous quote for goodness sake!)

"Define your business goals clearly so that others can see them as you do!"

–George F. Burns

We have tried to figure out for years why people do not set goals and for the life of us we can only come up with a few reasons why they don't...

They do not know how...or

They do not think it will help...or

They just do not care!

It has been proven by scientific studies, college research, and spouses all across the country, people who set goals have a 98% more successful sales career, than those who do not. Now granted, that 85% of statistics are completely made up on the spot, but who cares? The bottom line is that if you would take the time to set out some goals, you will be amazed at what will happen!

Setting goals is kind of like having a plan, but setting goals are specific targets that you want to reach. A goal would be something like, I want to make 15 sales per month, and a plan would be the strategy on how to achieve the goal.

But it is not just setting the goal itself that is enough. You have to write your goals down, review them regularly, and measure your progress. The last thing you need to do is to write down a bunch of goals and stick that paper in a drawer never to look at it again. What good is that? Not much, but plenty of people do!

Goals need to be large enough to require hard work to reach them, but not so far out of reach that you can never attain them.

Here is the good news. We have put together a goal setting worksheet just for you! You can go get your free copy right now at www.themarketingevangelist.com/dude

Print it out and make plenty of copies. Don't be afraid to set what we call a BHAG. That is a Big Hairy Audacious Goal as well. That is a goal, that if you achieve it, you will feel as if you have won the Power Ball Lotto!

You Do Not Track Your Goals!

Tim and Nick's Famous Quote Validation!
(Because we figure that if you don't believe us, maybe you will believe a famous quote for goodness sake!)

"A goal without a plan is just a wish!"
-Antoine de Saint-Exupery

Have you ever heard the statement, "what gets measured, gets done"? The sad truth is that very few sales people actually track the progress of their goals; hence, they are broke. If you want to make more money in sales, after you get some goals, you need to start tracking your progress.

The chances are that at some point you actually did write your goals down and then you stuffed that sheet into a drawer somewhere. Putting your goals in a drawer and never looking at them is about as good as buying groceries and never eating them. Every now and then you need to go to the refrigerator, open the door, and see what you have left! That is the same with your goals!

The sales profession has often been called a numbers game. If you talk to x number of people, then you will make x number of sales. The question is what is that number for you? If you track your goals, then you will improve your closing ratio. If you need to see or talk to 100 people in order to make just one sale, then you need to visit your sales skills.

Your goals can not be in your head! They must be on paper! If we had a nickel for every time we asked someone about their goals and they told us they didn't have them written down, we would be flat out gazillionaires! In order for you to achieve the success you say you want you need to do four things…

1. Identify your goals! Know your numbers!
2. Write them down!
3. Review them daily and measure your progress!
4. Make adjustments!

Now telling you this is one thing, but we are also going to provide you we our goal tracking worksheet! All you need to do is go to http://www.themarketingevangelist.com/dude and enter your name and email and we will instantly send you this form! You can start using it right away!

You Expect People to Buy From You, But You Dress Like Your Homeless!

Tim and Nick's Famous Quote Validation!
(Because we figure that if you don't believe us, maybe you will believe a famous quote for goodness sake!)

"You have to dress up if you want to go up!"

– Zig Ziglar

Dude, Seriously! It's the 21st Century and there's a new invention called **AN IRON**, use it! Have you ever heard the saying, "image is everything" or "perception is reality"? What are you being perceived as, a success or a failure? Who do you want business from, a CEO or a homeless guy? Your attire tells a story long before you open your mouth. Does the way you dress say you belong to be there?

It is critical that you dress for your audience. You can even have a uniform if you like. Plenty of people identify themselves with a uniform. But if you do that, make sure it is washed and pressed. Here are some tips for business dress for those of you who may not have or desire a uniform.

For the Dudes…

- Iron your clothes, or get them dry cleaned!
- Make sure your tie touches the top of your belt buckle!
- Make sure your tie is not too short or too long!
- A sports coat will dress up casual clothes!
- Your belt and shoes should be the same color!

For the Dudettes…

- There's a time and a place for cleavage and unless it's on the cover of a magazine, work isn't the place!
- You wear the makeup, the makeup doesn't wear you!
- High heels boost your posture and polish any outfit, just make sure you can walk in them!

If you find that you are wardrobe challenged, then many department stores have personal shoppers that can help you find the right clothes that fit. If they do not have a personal shopper, then the mannequin is a great place to start. Just look at the mannequin and find the same outfit.

You Never Take Action!

Tim and Nick's Famous Quote Validation!
(Because we figure that if you don't believe us, maybe you will believe a famous quote for goodness sake!)

"Action conquers fear!"
–Author Unknown

Haven't we already covered this in the chapter, You Over Think Everything? Yes, but it is important enough to cover is again. You see, we believe that knowledge is just a bunch of garbage, unless you take that knowledge and do something with it! Nick and I have met a lot of sales people who always have another great idea, or they or going to really do something fantastic, or they have yet another plan…

All of these are good, but if you really want to be great, you are going to have to take some action. Do something! Make a phone call, send a letter, or go to a networking function, but for Pete's sake do something!

If you are sitting behind your desk, waiting for the phone to ring, then you are really sitting there waiting to go bankrupt! We really like Zig Ziglar and he once said that "motion creates emotion…" He is completely right. Action conquers fear and leads you toward achieving your goals, now that you are going to write them down and start tracking how you are doing. (just a little accountability for you, to make sure you take action!)

Taking action requires that you identify an action, set a target date for accomplishing the action and either hold yourself accountable, or have someone hold you accountable for the task!

Take a moment to answer these questions…

1. What is the one thing you know you need to do, but have not done yet?
2. When can you get started?
3. What is the first step you need to take?
4. When is your deadline for accomplishing this task?

Getting started is hard, but keeping the momentum can be even harder. The good news is that taking action will eliminate any fears and doubts you have and will really start to make you feel better. When you feel good, your sales will improve!

You Are Ashamed of What You Sell and Don't Even Use it Yourself!

Tim and Nick's Famous Quote Validation!

(Because we figure that if you don't believe us, maybe you will believe a famous quote for goodness sake!)

"Live in such a way that you would not be ashamed to sell your parrot to the town gossip!"

–Will Rogers

"Hi, I hate my job and I hate this product. Would you please buy from me?" Seriously! That's what you say with your body language, tone of voice and lack of professionalism when you don't use your own product or are ashamed of what you do!.

How can you expect anyone to buy anything from you if you don't believe in your product or are ashamed of what you do? Your ability to sell is directly tied to your passion level for what you do and your belief in your product.

Your enthusiasm is the telling sign to your potential buyer of what you honestly think about your product.

Enthusiasm, passion, and attitude are all very contagious. You need to make sure that yours are all worth catching.

Your potential buyer needs to feel and completely understand your passion and that your life's calling is to spread the word on how great your product or service is. If you don't feel this way, then perhaps you should find another career, sales may not be for you.

Selling is a career that requires a high level of self respect and self esteem. If you can't convey this to your potential buyer, then either you're selling the wrong product, shouldn't be in sales, or perhaps you need to take inventory or your sales presentation and realize that you have missed some key features of your product and how it can solve certain problems for your buyers. Don't miss a sale by leaving your passion at home.

Here are some tips to help you make the most of every selling opportunity!

Be passionate about your product!

Be passionate about what you do!

Don't assume you know what the potential buyer is looking for, ask the right questions!

You Do Not Plan for the Future!

Tim and Nick's Famous Quote Validation!

(Because we figure that if you don't believe us, maybe you will believe a famous quote for goodness sake!)

"Treasure your relationships, not your possessions!"

–Anthony J. D'Angelo

Dude, Seriously! Have you ever heard someone say, "Where have the years gone"? It's easy in today's age of hustle bustle to sacrifice the future for the urgent issues at hand.

In sales it is vital to your well being to push beyond the day to day task and plan for where you want to be in 5, 10, or even 20 years. It's so easy to wake up each day and set out to look under rocks to find out where your next check is coming from, but is that what you want to be doing in 20 years?

If not then set up a plan to where you can strategically position yourself to live a better life 20 years from now. In sales life, you should never become complacent with where you are today. Look confidently towards the future and go after it with everything you got!

The minute you stop planning for the future and striving for it, is the minute you lose your edge and sabotage your career and potentially your life. We heard someone once say that "if you aim for nothing you'll probably get there". You only get one shot at life, make the most of it. Write your life's story and go out and live it.

Helpful Hints:

- Consider where you want to be in 30 yrs and what you want to be doing.
- Each day take one small step in that direction. You won't regret it, but you will regret it if you don't!
- Start a savings account today! We don't care if you start with 1 dollar or ten thousand dollars! Just start!
- Start eliminating your debt right now! The more debt you have the more you will struggle in sales!
- Put up pictures of where you want to retire, the lifestyle you want, and anything else to keep you motivated to getting to your future goal!

You Do Not Ask for Referrals!

Tim and Nick's Famous Quote Validation!
(Because we figure that if you don't believe us, maybe you will believe a famous quote for goodness sake!)

"You have not because you ask not!"
–James 4:2

The absolute best time to get referrals is during the sales process with a current client, so why don't you ask for them? If you are afraid, then get over it. If you don't believe in your product, then get a new one. But for Pete's sake, you have to start asking for referrals!

Did you know that 87% of people polled said they would be happy to provide a referral, but they were never asked! Are you kidding us??? You can have more referral business if you just ask! Wow, that certainly takes the guess work out of the puzzle, doesn't it?

But the truth is that just simply asking for a referral isn't really enough. People have to be precisely directed to who they can refer to you. Here is exactly how you do this…

You have to give them specific people at specific places to get them to think! Why?-because people's minds are like a picture rolodex. If all you say is, "By the way if you know anyone who needs my product or service, be sure to give them my card" then the answer you will always get is this…"You bet, I sure will!" But you know what happens next?

Nothing, zip, zilch, notta!! You think you did the right thing, but if you don't actually get a referral, you really just ran your mouth.

Here is exactly how you fix this problem and get more referrals. Say this…

"You know I really appreciate your business, and I was wondering if you know anyone at work or church that could use my product or service?"

Did you notice the difference? You are specifically asking them to think about a specific person at a specific place. People will automatically dial up their mental picture rolodex and process to see if there is anyone that they can refer you. If you use this simple technique, your referrals will go up 100%!

You Think that Your Company Owes You Something!

Tim and Nick's Famous Quote Validation!

(Because we figure that if you don't believe us, maybe you will believe a famous quote for goodness sake!)

"Opportunities are usually disguised as hard work, so most people do not recognize them!"

–Ann Landers

If you think that your company owes you something then you are really messed up. They owe you nothing. They have given you an opportunity and what you do with that opportunity is completely up to you. We hear sales people all the time complain about their companies. Good grief, if it is that bad then quit. Here are some of the most common complaints we hear...

My company doesn't provide any training! (Have you read our chapter on investing in yourself? If yes, then re-read it now and if you have not read it, then go read it now.)

My company doesn't provide leads. (Really, you want leads? You are in sales. Go find them. Network, ask, but for Pete's sake leave the office!)

My company doesn't provide me enough paid time off. (Here is a tip, if you make enough sales, and save enough money, then you can take time off. And on a side note, they are not in business to pay for vacations. They are in business to make a profit! Your job is to help in that area!)

My company doesn't have great benefits. (Seriously, the days of company matching 401k are dwindling rapidly. It is your job to take care of you and your family! If you make enough sales, save more and spend less, then you will have enough money!)

At the end of the day, your job is to get up each and every day to give your family, yourself, and your company your very best. The Bible says it this way in Deuteronomy 8:18 But remember the Lord your God, for it is He who gives YOU the ability to produce wealth...

After all our research the Bible never said that God gives the company the ability – He give YOU the ability. You just need to get off your butt, stop thinking about what the company "owes you", start focusing on your sales goals, and take daily action to get the results you want!

You Are Chronically Late for Appointments!

Tim and Nick's Famous Quote Validation!

(Because we figure that if you don't believe us, maybe you will believe a famous quote for goodness sake!)

"Tardiness often robs us of opportunity, and the dispatch of our forces!"

–Niccolo Machiavelli

Dude, seriously! Showing up late to a sales meeting is a sure fire way to kill the deal and your career!

You work so hard to get business, set yourself apart from everyone else and then when you show up late to meet your potential client for an appointment what you are really saying to them is, *"Mr. Client, I really don't need your business. I've got more important clients than you and more important things to do than to serve you. But I'll give you my left over time. I don't respect you and I really don't want to earn your business."*

"So Mr. Client, since I'm late to the appointment, you can count on being my last priority day in and day out. In the future, please don't expect a high level of service or professionalism from me because you're not that important – however I still need for you to pay my price, that's fair isn't it?"

So what can you do to prevent this disaster? Here are some of our best tips…

- Leave earlier! You don't know what traffic will be like so give yourself enough time!
- If you are going somewhere you have never been, then drive there the day before!
- Check out www.mapquest.com print out a map, it will do you some good!

Plan on arriving 15 minutes early! If you are there early, here are some things you can do…

- Make a note of there office or facilities. Look for things of common interest or family photos that you can bring up in the conversation!
- Build rapport with the receptionist! They are usually the gatekeeper, so if you get on their good side, then you are a shoe in for future visits!
- Review your sales presentation. You can never practice this enough!

You Do Not Return Calls Promptly!

Tim and Nick's Famous Quote Validation!
(Because we figure that if you don't believe us, maybe you will believe a famous quote for goodness sake!)

"Time is money!"
– Benjamin Franklin

No one ever calls you wanting to get your voice mail! When they call, they want to talk to you. Now the truth is that you can not take every call, every time. You have meetings, sales presentations, and other task to do. But for Heavens sake, you need to return your calls promptly.

The first step is that your voice mail should set the proper expectations with the caller. Everyone says something like, "you have reached so and so and I am sorry I can't take your call, but if you leave me your name and number I will call you back as soon as possible…"

Our question is "when is that?" Is "as soon as possible" today, tomorrow, or next week? Who knows? Chances are you don't even know and that is because you don't have a set schedule of what you are going to do. If you are ever going to change your career, you are going to have to set a schedule and stick to it!

We have a suggestion…

Change your voice mail and set a schedule!

Here is a script that we have been using for years that sets the proper expectations, generates referrals, and creates more stability in your career.

"Hi you have reached (your name). You have reached me at a time I have scheduled for meetings with clients. I do return calls in the morning between ---- and ---- and I return afternoon calls between ---- and ----. If you will leave me the best number to reach you during these times I will return your call today. Don't forget to ask me about (insert a special or promotion here)"

This simple script has changed the lives of many sales people. People will respect your time and work with you when you do what you say you will do and give them proper expectations. We like to call it controlling your day versus letting the tail wag the dog.

Now that you have a specific strategy for your voice mail, the only thing you need to do is actually return the calls! They just may be trying to put cash in your pocket!

You Do Not Have a Clear Sales Presentation and Worse Yet You Are Unprepared!

Tim and Nick's Famous Quote Validation!
(Because we figure that if you don't believe us, maybe you will believe a famous quote for goodness sake!)

"I am prepared to meet anyone, but whether anyone is prepared for the great ordeal of meeting me is another matter!"

–Mark Twain

Admit it! You probably do not have a visual sales presentation do you? Notice we said visual presentation. Most sales people we meet just start rambling on about their product or service, like we are going to really remember much of what you said...unless you have a crystal clear, money making unique selling proposition, which in our experience few have. That is just one reason for having a visual sales presentation.

But you may be saying, "what the heck is a visual presentation?" A visual presentation is most likely a flip chart or book that allows you to walk your prospect through the entire buying process. Why do you need one? Two reasons...

1. So you don't screw things up and lose the sale and,
2. Because people are mostly visual learners and seeing what you are explaining gives them a clear roadmap that can help them make the decision.

When you just talk and talk and talk, you are leaving the visual up to them. You hope that they are engaged, but in reality they could be thinking about anything from a golf shot, to last night's episode of Big Brother. Do you really want to leave your commission up to chance like that? Your paycheck could be riding on your product or who got voted out of the Big Brother house.

If you leave it up to your verbal skills and their mental skills, then they could end up becoming confused. The problem with people who are confused is this...a confused mind will ALWAYS say no. We can't afford too many no's and neither can you.

So do yourself and your business a favor. Draw out your sales process. Make sure you have plenty of visuals and a road map that you and your customer can follow. Simple? Yes! And simple always works!

You Never Read Any Books!

Tim and Nick's Famous Quote Validation!

(Because we figure that if you don't believe us, maybe you will believe a famous quote for goodness sake!)

"The man who does not read good books has no advantage over the man who can't read them"

–Mark Twain

Dude, Seriously! You don't read books! Obviously growing up in school, reading was of no value. You were able to increase your knowledge and your vocabulary year over year in school simply by aging.

In the competitive age we life in today, the difference between winning the sale and losing to a competitor is razor thin. There are number of reason why it is crucial to your development as a professional to read. Reading obviously brings with it an increase in knowledge, but also it will provide different sales techniques and a better vocabulary.

If you don't know sales strategies that have proven successful, you can't use them. If knowledge is power, then increase your knowledge of the sales skill and use it! There is so much information out there to help you identify what techniques and approaches work with different personality types and how to effectively communicate to make sure your clients arrive at a **BUYING** decision.

Reading books will help provide you with good insight to different sales systems and strategies necessary to increase your closing ratio. Plus it is good for your mind!

Here are some of our recommended books:

The Bible

7 Habits of Highly Effective People by Stephen R. Covey

Little Red Book of Selling by Jeffrey Gitomer

You Were Created for Greatness by CJ Small (greatness12.com)

You Were Born to Be an Original, Don't Live Like a Copy by Jonathan Sprinkles (www.jsprinkles.com)

We have more recommendation on our blog!

You Think You Know it All!

Tim and Nick's Famous Quote Validation!

(Because we figure that if you don't believe us, maybe you will believe a famous quote for goodness sake!)

"I not only use all the brains that I have, but all that I can borrow!"

–Woodrow Wilson

The minute you think you have it all figured out, is the minute that you are getting ready for a huge fall. In fact, we don't even believe we have it all figured out. We are always looking for inspiration, creation, and motivation! Your mind is the biggest battle you will ever face and never let your mind tell you that you know it all.

The very best sales people in the world are always seeking out knowledge. We have met countless sales people who believe that they know it all, but their bank accounts sure don't reflect that they know anything.

We recently even had someone send us a written comment that said the following…

"If a man need s coaching- he;s probably either no motivated or in the wrong profession."

Now the sad part is that, the grammar that was used in the initial e-mail was so bad, that we put it in the book exactly how it was written. This person is an idiot because of two reasons…

1. They made a comment that is completely ridiculous and,
2. They need a grammar coach really bad!

This is an obvious example of exactly what we are talking about. The world is changing rapidly. The way business has been done in the past is not necessarily how it will be done in the future and you need to always stay on top of your business and technology. This is really great news for successful sales people because they understand that knowledge plus action equals power.

So you need to go out and arm yourself with knowledge by subscribing to your industries trade magazines and websites. You also need to load up your audio library with sales and motivational messages as well.

We have always said that it only takes one idea to change your life. Cinderella said it this way…"one shoe can change your life." Your job is to be looking for the shoe!

You Think Networking Groups Are a Waste of Time!

Tim and Nick's Famous Quote Validation!
(Because we figure that if you don't believe us, maybe you will believe a famous quote for goodness sake!)

"Treasure your relationships, not your possessions!"
–Anthony J. D'Angelo

Structured networking groups like BNI (www.bni.com) and LeTip (www.letip.com) are a great way to build your business, but they do not work just because you show up. Showing up is just your ticket in the front door. We have heard sales people all the time say that these groups are a waste of time and do not produce results. Bologna! The cliché that says…"you get out of it what you put into it" really applies in this area!

Here are the biggest mistakes sales people make with their structured networking groups…

1. They are not committed to the group!
2. The do not have a clearly defined sixty second commercial that gets the massive referrals!
3. They fail to develop one on one relationship's with members of the group!
4. They never give and are always looking to take!

Networking is a fundamental tool for success in the world of sales! Networking is all about building relationships and at the very root of every successful sales person is a gigantic rolodex of relationships!

If you are afraid to go to networking groups, then maybe sales is not for you, but if you are ready to fast forward your sales, here are some tips to know about choosing the right networking group.

1. You have to interview the people in the group. These people are ultimately going to be your commission free sales force, looking to refer you business. If they are a big group of slackers, then you will never get business! Think of it like hiring, if you would hire them to sale for you then you are in the right group!
2. Look for groups with structure. Groups that follow a clearly defined process, set goals, and hold their member accountable, will always out perform any other loosely knit group.

You Take Sales Advice From Broke Sales People!

Tim and Nick's Famous Quote Validation!

(Because we figure that if you don't believe us, maybe you will believe a famous quote for goodness sake!)

"Advice is judged by results, not by intentions!"

–Cicero

Dude, Seriously! Are you kidding me! This is vital to your business. I'm sure you've realized that everyone wants to put their two cents worth in on your career. And most people, if we're being real honest, love to hear themselves talk, especially sales people.

Remember you are who you hang around and that applies to business. If you take advice from people that aren't successful then that's exactly what you will become. If you surround yourself with unsuccessful people, you will begin to think and act like them.

Now lets turn the table, If Iron sharpens iron as the Bible indicates, then surround yourself with successful sales people. Success leaves the clues for you to grab hold of and put into practice in your own life!

Whenever we have wanted to become inspired or create something in our business, the first place we turn to is our list of successful friends. We may bounce ideas off them, read and listen to some of their messages, or join one of their coaching groups. We know that if we get just one idea, then take action, that maybe, just maybe, we will have huge results!

One of the many benefits from looking to successful people for advice you're able to use their proven strategies and ideas and let them lead the way for your success.

Tips

- Identify unsuccessful people currently in your life you need to discount their advice or separate yourself from. Who do you know right now?
- Seek out successful people to surround yourself with. What groups can you join?
- Be open minded and attentive when someone successful is giving you ideas. Take the ideas and then take action. You may be surprised at the results you will get!

You Complain All the Time!

Tim and Nick's Famous Quote Validation!
(Because we figure that if you don't believe us, maybe you will believe a famous quote for goodness sake!)

"Any fool can criticize, condemn and complain – and most fools do!"
–Dale Carnegie

Complaining will get you kicked out of the check deposit line and sent straight to the soup line...but eventually they will even kick you out of that line! There is nothing worse than a complaining sales person. It turns off your co-workers, your vendors, and most importantly your customers.

Complaining is different from making excuses, because complaining usually starts out with the word "my". Excuses are usually blaming someone else or some external force for your failure, but complaining is really just an attitude.

Here is our top 10 list of complaints that sales people make.

1. My pay is too low.
2. My leads are crap.
3. My work is hard.
4. My customers are rude.
5. My product is bad.
6. My manager is mean.
7. My assistant is slow.
8. My company sucks.
9. My vendors are slow.
10. My vacation time is too short.

We hear this all the time from really bad sales people. So we have come up with a three step program for salvation from complaining...

Step 1: Change Your Attitude

Step 2: Change Your Attitude

Step 3: If Step 1 or 2 does not work, then find a new career where complaining is acceptable. (We do not know where that is, so you may need to revisit step one and two.)

You Show Up Late and Leave Early!

Tim and Nick's Famous Quote Validation!

(Because we figure that if you don't believe us, maybe you will believe a famous quote for goodness sake!)

"The trouble with being punctual is that nobody is there to appreciate it!"

–Franklin P. Jones

Dude, Seriously! The biggest mistake people in sales do is showing up late and leaving early. We have seen sales people with great potential never get off the starting blocks because they set themselves up for failure by not putting in full day's work.

In sales, although typically you are in control of your schedule, by design you should be using it to generate sales. Sales people who don't have a regular set work hours - sleep late, look for reasons during the day to avoid work, and typically leave early.

Remember, it's not the hours you are on a job, but income producing activities you completed during the day and task completed to reach your goals that count. On the other hand, sales professionals that have a set work day realize that arriving late or leaving early is only cheating themselves' and will lead to their failure.

Remember, in sales you have the opportunity to control your schedule, use it to your advantage. If you don't, you'll end up working somewhere that controls your schedule for you.

If you do not have a schedule, then the here is a picture of what your sales will look like…

(this space left intentionally blank)

You See People as Dollar Signs and Not Life Time Relationships!

Tim and Nick's Famous Quote Validation!
(Because we figure that if you don't believe us, maybe you will believe a famous quote for goodness sake!)

"If you will make a friend first, then you will make a sale!"
–Tim Davis & Nick Thomas

Ok, we cheated and threw our own quote in, but you know it's true!

We recently recorded an interview with Denai Vaughn (www.thenetworkingqueen.net) and she was telling us the story of how she had received a call from a person she met at a networking event. She said that from the minute she said hello, the person went into complete sales mode. Denai didn't even have a chance to get a word in edge wise.

We can not stress this enough. If you are all about the money and not about the relationships then your business is doomed for failure. It may not happen at first, but trust us in this, at some point you will need business and unless you have invested in relationships, you will be struggling at best and out of business at worse. Investing in people is one of the best investments you will ever make. People want a chance to be heard, and they really want a chance to feel valuable. Are you making your customers feel valuable? Or do your customers think that you are only in it for the money?

So what do you do to make sure you have a My Customer is the Most Valuable Person on the Planet strategy? Here are some tips…

1. Get to know them on a personal level. You need to know what they like, their favorite sports team, their kids and family, and who they really are as a person.
2. Send them things to let them know you care. We recommend handwritten cards that say "I really care about you as a person!"
3. Call them just to say hi and not for a sales call.

We have developed a strategy called The Customer Concierge Business Builder. It is a simple form that helps you collect all the really important stuff to people. We combine this with our www.maximumsalesgenerator.com database tool, and when you put the two of these together, business explodes! It comes down to this, people don't care how much you know, until they know how much you care!

You Do Not Take Care of Your Health!

Tim and Nick's Famous Quote Validation!

(Because we figure that if you don't believe us, maybe you will believe a famous quote for goodness sake!)

"Health is not valued until sickness comes!"

–Dr. Thomas Fuller

Dude, Seriously! You don't take care of your health! Maybe you think you're still in college living the dream, pizza and buffalo wings for breakfast lunch and dinner. Take it from a guy with one kidney, as a sales professional need to take care of your health to keep your sales skills at the highest level possible, along with the obvious reasons for your family and loved ones. Maybe you haven't noticed how your diet determines how you feel and how much energy you have as quick as 30 minutes after you eat.

You need to have the eye of the tiger desire for sales burning in you at all times, and you can't have that when the majority of your blood is in your stomach aiding in digestion when it should be in your head being creative. Your body operates best on 6 small meals a day rather than 2 to 3 big meals. The more calories you take in per sitting, the more energy your body takes to digest it. Do yourself a favor and eat light meals during the day every 3-4 hours to keep your body and mind at peak performance rather than tired and lethargic during the day when you need to be in peak sales performance.

Also, It has been proven that getting your heart rate up once a day for 30 minutes in a cardiovascular workout helps release stress and produces endorphins that help you think clearer and fight off depression.

Hints:

- ✓ Exercise 4-5 times a week getting your heart rate up for 30 minutes per time.
- ✓ Decrease the portions of your meals to around 300 to 400 calories per meal 5-6 times per day based on activity level.
- ✓ Remember, some people don't have good heath to take care of and wish they had the opportunity to be in your shoes.

You Do Not Control You're your Thoughts and Emotions!

Tim and Nick's Famous Quote Validation!

(Because we figure that if you don't believe us, maybe you will believe a famous quote for goodness sake!)

"Your attitude, not your aptitude, will determine your altitude!"

–Zig Ziglar

Controlling your attitude and emotions is critical to your success in the world of sales. Why is it so critical? Because people are going to tell you no, shut the door in your face, and not return your calls. Prospects will avoid you, gatekeepers will block you, and your best direct mail piece will not give you the return you had expected.

So that being said, what will you do when all of this happens? If you let it get you down, then you are toast. Your mind is the biggest battle you will face. Day in and day out, your mind will try and convince you to not make the call, not knock on the next door, and just blow off the day. If you give in, then you are sabotaging your career!

You would not think of not eating for a whole week, yet many sales people will not feed their mind daily! Getting positive is easy, staying positive requires work.

But just feeding your mind positive information is not just for you. Sure it helps keep you hopeful for the next victory, but it does something much more…

Keeping your attitude positive, keeps your customers positive. Let's face it, if your attitude is in the toilet, then your customers will pick up on a poor attitude faster than a tick on a dog. (Yes we are from Nashville, and are allowed to say that in a book.) If your clients think your attitude is poor they may not buy from you at least, and at worse, they will tell everyone else to stay clear of you and your business.

The bottom line is this:

1. You must control your attitude for yourself and your health and,
2. You must control your attitude for your current and future clients.

Why? Because your sales depend on it! And if you need an extra boost, then you should check out www.mondayinspiration.com You can get a personal phone call each Monday that will motivate, encourage and inspire you. That is just what the doctor ordered!

You Strive for Mediocrity!

Tim and Nick's Famous Quote Validation!
(Because we figure that if you don't believe us, maybe you will believe a famous quote for goodness sake!)

"I am easily satisfied with the very best!"
–Winston Churchill

Dude, Seriously! You strive for mediocrity! That's great! We've seen all those self help books on helping people become average! We think a few of them are on the New York Times Best Sellers list! If being mediocre weren't satisfying enough, you never have to be let down by not reaching your goals or dreams, because you've decided to be mediocre. Congratulations! You've succeeded!

Striving for mediocrity is a quick path to your sales career demise. Becoming satisfied with being average will lead to burn out in your career and frustration because you will quickly lose passion for what you do. Sales require that you have a daily desire to get up and become fully involved in your career.

True successful sales professionals discipline themselves physically, mentally and emotionally to get up every day and go make it happen. It's much like the growth of your muscles, either you are increasing the strength of your muscles or they become weak. Choose to intentionally strive for success, purposefully control your thoughts to strive for more.

Helpful Hints:

- ✓ You are who you hang around. Surround yourself with people that are constantly striving for success!

- ✓ Stop spending time with complacent people with no desire or discipline to succeed!

- ✓ Fill your mind with positive motivational words through success coaches, motivational speeches, and motivational books!

- ✓ Have fun and concentrate on reaching your maximum potential! It will be good for you and great for the people you love!

You Do Not Try New Things!

Tim and Nick's Famous Quote Validation!

(Because we figure that if you don't believe us, maybe you will believe a famous quote for goodness sake!)

"If you are not willing to risk the unusual, you will have to settle for the ordinary!"

–Jim Rohn

Business is moving so fast, it is almost impossible to keep up, but we see sales people all the time keep doing the same things over and over again that produce no results. Take networking for example. We see people go to networking groups, but they get no business. When we approach them about changing their message, they resist.

We have all heard that the definition of insanity is doing the same thing over and over again and expecting different results. If what you are doing is not resulting in sales, then you need to try something new.

We have a good friend who had been getting amazing results from his email marketing campaign for several years. As he continued to track and measure his results, he was finding the response rates were trailing off. He tried tweaking the copy, frequency, and design of the newsletters, but nothing he did seemed to work. We consulted with him about doing video marketing.

At first he was reluctant, but gave it a shot. You know what happen? Sales went through the roof! Now we have given this idea to many other clients who continue to be resistant to trying something new. Guess what…their sales are still in the toilet.

There is not one magic bullet that will work forever. You have to try new things. Your market demands new things. Resist and suffer the fatal blow to your bank account.

Here is a list of some new "things" to try, if you are not too chicken…

- Video Marketing!
- Social Media Marketing!
- Giving speeches, seminars, or talks!
- Writing a book! Don't smirk, you can do this!
- Writing articles for magazines and newspapers!

Never underestimate your potential! You will be amazed at what you can accomplish when you just try!

You Think Facebook is A Fad!

Tim and Nick's Famous Quote Validation!

(Because we figure that if you don't believe us, maybe you will believe a famous quote for goodness sake!)

"Facebook truly is a modern phenomenon; a virtual meeting place with over 150,000,000 users and a marketer's paradise where you can attract a catalog of 5000 friends at warp speed!"

We meet people all the time that are not using www.facebook.com and for the life of us we can't figure out why. Over one million people are signing up every week to this free social networking site. The amount of opportunities' is simply mind boggling! We have even heard that if facebook was a country it would be the 35th largest country in the world. We don't know if that's true, but good grief, with the amount of people signing up, it sure could be!

There are some common mistakes that people in sales make on facebook. Here are just a few...

- Spamming your sales message in every post. You have to make friends to make sales.
- Not being active enough. If you implement this strategy, then make sure you commit to its success!
- Posting too much. You don't have the time and people don't care to hear from you every 5 minutes. Chill.
- Never taking the online, offline. Relationships are formed by meetings, and phone calls. Never let technology replace personal interaction!
- Not putting up your photo. Come on people we want to see ya for crying out loud!

We like to refer to facebook as the virtual chamber of commerce. You can meet so many people and make so many connections that can make a real difference in your business.

We have also been told that some business won't allow their sales staff to use facebook. That is stupid and if you are in a company like that, maybe you need to have your boss read our book and then give us a call. We would be happy to train your company on Successful Sales Strategies in Social Networking! *And on a side note, you can find us on facebook, so be sure to send us a friend request! Just look up Tim Davis or Nick Thomas!*

You Hate Change!

Tim and Nick's Famous Quote Validation!
(Because we figure that if you don't believe us, maybe you will believe a famous quote for goodness sake!)

"Change your thoughts and you will change your world!"
–Norman Vincent Peale

Dude, seriously! Yeah, you don't need to change, why would I start using in IPOD when I can use my 8 track! Change is inevitable and change is probably the most consistent thing you can count on in the world today! The problem with people who don't embrace change is that all they will have in their pocket will be loose change. Change always comes down to a matter of perspective. If you have a negative view of the change, then you will get bogged down and defeated…

But on the other hand, if you look at the change and ask yourself how this can be turned into an opportunity, then you are on the right track! The biggest windfalls have occurred not because of change, but because of the perspective of the change.

Your perspective is really all about how you view the situation. You have heard people say, "they see the glass half empty, or they see the glass half full…" if you want to have the right perspective, then you need to see the glass running over! Tony Robins said, "nothing is either good or bad, but it's how we perceive it". Perspective is your most valuable asset when it comes to change. Do yourself a favor and learn to embrace it.

Here are some great questions to help you see the change as a tremendous opportunity!

1. How can this change result in more opportunity?
2. How can this change help me solve a client's problem?
3. How can I take the current change and create a new product or service for my clients?
4. How does this change impact my competitors?
5. How can the change result in gaining market share?

You Have No Passion!

Tim and Nick's Famous Quote Validation!

(Because we figure that if you don't believe us, maybe you will believe a famous quote for goodness sake!)

"Live with Passion" and

"Passion is the genesis of genius!" – Tony Robbins

We really have absolutely no clue as to how you can be really successful if you do not have passion for your career, your customers, and your product. Passion sells, even when the sales person has absolutely zero sales skills.

Nick and I worked hard at coming up with a solution to help you get passionate about your career and here is the formula we came found…

NOTHING!

That's right. We do not know how to teach you passion. You either are working in a career you are passionate about or you are not. We know a lot of sales people who make great money, but hate their jobs. If you are one of those people, then you need to find something you love to do and then find a way to get paid for doing it. Life is just too short to not live with passion!

Success is not just money, possessions, or stuff…real success comes from contributing to others and leaving a legacy for people to follow. We all have something that we love to do and it is most often that thing that you would do for free. Whatever it is in life that you would do for free, that is your passion!

Now, do not get passion confused with obsession! We do not need any more obsessed people running around. What this world really needs are passionate people with a purpose.

Take our passion test to determine how passionate you are about your career…

On a scale of 1-10, with 10 being "red hot" please rate yourself on the following question…

I love my job so much I would take a 50% pay cut and not lose any desire or passion.

How did you do? If you are between 8 and 10, then congratulations! If you are 7 or below, then you need to think about why that is.

You Do Not Know Your Product!

Tim and Nick's Famous Quote Validation!

(Because we figure that if you don't believe us, maybe you will believe a famous quote for goodness sake!)

"Study to show yourself approved" – God, 2 Timothy 2:15

Product knowledge is critical to your success because it is a fundamental component of confidence. We have no clue as to how you will ever be successful in sales unless you decide to be enthusiastic about learning your product. In other words, you need to become a student of the game. One of the keys to this area is that you will need to have a desire to seek out the knowledge on your own. If you work for a company that provides training, then that is a huge bonus, but the really top notch sales professionals are always looking to know more about their product. They will go beyond the company training and do a lot of self education.

In our past careers, we have won countless sales because of product knowledge. That product knowledge showed up in our conversations and created a sense of security in the client. People want to know that you can handle the job. They need to be certain that you will not drop the ball and the best way to show them, is through your product knowledge. You are always going to have competition, so you need to out-wit, out-smart, and out-compete them using your knowledge.

Gaining product knowledge is only half the battle, though. The other half is how to you communicate your knowledge in a way that you customer understands what the heck you are saying so that they will buy your product or service. You do that through taking the knowledge and breaking it down to a level so that even a third grader can understand. One of our fundamental rules of selling is that a confused mind will always say no. Your job is to get rid of the confusion. Here are our tips to gaining knowledge and using it to influence your customer.

1. Make a decision to dedicate yourself to gaining knowledge. Self education is always the best, because you choose to gain it!
2. Take industry jargon and break it down to a third grade level and use analogies to help your customer understand and say yes!

You Do Not Listen to Your Customers!

Tim and Nick's Famous Quote Validation!

(Because we figure that if you don't believe us, maybe you will believe a famous quote for goodness sake!)

"Successful people ask better questions and as a result get better results!"

–Tony Robbins

Do you remember that song: We don't need no education? There is a line in there that says, "How can you have your pudding if you don't eat your meat?" That really applies to sales people everywhere. How can you possibly expect to sell something if you are the one doing all the talking! At some point you have to ask a great question, and be willing to shut up, so your client can answer.

An amazing thing will begin to happen…your clients will actually clue you in on how to sell to them! If you ask the right questions, you will uncover their problems and concerns. When they tell you their problems, then and only then, can you provide the right solution!

The right message, delivered at the right time, will always produce the right results. How you get to the right message is through listening.

We see sales people fumble all the time because they start blabbering about features and benefits that their clients could care less about. Sure your product has great features, and sure your product has great benefits, but your customer only cares about the ones that directly solve their problem.

We love problems. If we can find the problem, we know we can find the solution. Here are some really great questions for you to ask you clients…

1. What is your biggest concern right now?
2. If you could have one thing that would cure your biggest problem, what would that be?
3. What struggles are you having right now in your business?

Once you let your customer talk (and we mean let them talk) you will be amazed at what they reveal to you! When you really know their problem you can solve their need.

Hello, are you hearing us? Is this thing on?

You Do Not Ask for the Business!

Tim and Nick's Famous Quote Validation!

(Because we figure that if you don't believe us, maybe you will believe a famous quote for goodness sake!)

"You are never guaranteed next year. People ask what you think of next season, you have to seize the opportunities when they're in front of you."

–Brett Farve

Dude, Seriously…when was the last time you asked for the business? Now this is a little different than asking for referrals, because what we are talking about making the first sale to a customer.

To put this in a little better perspective, the best selling book of all time, The Bible says this…

"You do not have, because you do not ask." For those of you who need to verify this, just go find a Bible and look up James 4:2.

We really do not know how to make it any more plain than that! If you want more sales, you have to ask! If you want an appointment with the decision maker, then you have to ask! Now some of you are saying, "what if they say no?" Some will, and that requires you to be persistent.

Now, when you ask, make sure you are specific about what you want. If you want a sale, ask for the sale.

Keep asking until they tell you to leave them alone or place a restraining order against you. You are in sales and that requires you to ask for business if you really want to be successful! Many years ago we worked in a company with 10 sales people. One of them in particular was a "pit bull" of sales. If he got your name and number, then you would hear from him until you bought or died! Now he wasn't rude, but he was persistent.

You have to learn to ask for the business and you have to be persistent in continuing to follow up. One of the most basis functions in sales is to simply just ask for the business. Here are some great questions to help you began asking for the business…

1. So, Mr/Mrs client are you ready to buy?
2. What is standing in the way from you buying today?

Actually, that is only one question we can recommend, but it is the right question to ask! Try it - you will be amazed by the results!

You Have a Fear of Failure!

Tim and Nick's Famous Quote Validation!
(Because we figure that if you don't believe us, maybe you will believe a famous quote for goodness sake!)

"In order to succeed, your desire for success should be greater than your fear of failure!"
–Bill Cosby

Yes you will fail. That is just how sales can be. Will you learn from your failure, get up, and try again is the real question!

We don't know if we can really say anything to make you feel better or get over the fear of failure, but what we do know is this…If you don't get over it, we will be forced to ridicule you in front of your friends.(just kidding)

Everyone has failed at one time or another. In fact, you have already failed. When you were a little baby, you tried to walk several times before you succeeded, but you never gave up. Why is that?-because at that age, you had not become conscious of failure. You didn't even know what the word was or what it meant.

It wasn't until you got older that your conscious had taken over and everything became so serious. We really don't believe that being afraid to fail is the real reason for not trying. We believe that it is really the fear of what others will say or think about you if you do try. At some point you need to learn that what others think really doesn't matter.

We tend to think that others think or talk about us a lot more than they really do. Sure they may say something negative. So what? There will always be those types of people around. The biggest fear you will ever have to overcome is the fear of what others may think.

We like the motto of…

Some will…Some won't…so what. You need to go with your gut and make things happen. If you really need to know that someone believes in you, then you can believe that we do. We believe that you can do great things, but you need to just do them.

One of our friends, Paul Dunn said that we all should take the Nike motto of just do it and apply it to our lives as ***just did it!***

You Have a Fear of Success!

Tim and Nick's Famous Quote Validation!

(Because we figure that if you don't believe us, maybe you will believe a famous quote for goodness sake!)

"Faith activates God - Fear activates the Enemy."

–Joel Olsteen

What would happen if your dreams really came true? Think about that for a moment. The following is a quote from the book, A Return to Love, by motivational speaker and author, Marianne Williamson. (www.marianne.com)

Our Deepest Fear

Our deepest fear is not that we are inadequate.
Our deepest fear is that we are powerful beyond measure.

It is our light, not our darkness, that most frightens us.
We ask ourselves, Who am I to be brilliant,
gorgeous, handsome, talented and fabulous?

Actually, who are you not to be?
You are a child of God.

Your playing small does not serve the world.
There is nothing enlightened about shrinking
so that other people won't feel insecure around you.
We are all meant to shine, as children do.

We were born to make manifest the glory of God within us.
It is not just in some; it is in everyone.

And, as we let our own light shine, we consciously give
other people permission to do the same.
As we are liberated from our fear,
our presence automatically liberates others.

So after you have read this, if you are still afraid of success, then all we can say is…

Dude, Seriously….

Perception is Reality! Here is who Nick and Tim use for their photography! Jason is the best and we highly recommend checking him out!

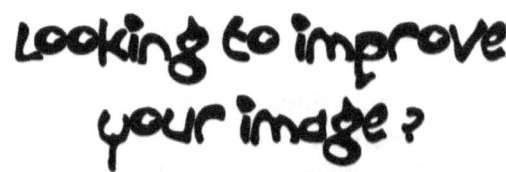

300 Donelson Pike
Nashville, TN 37214
(615) 874-0460
tuckerphotography.com

How Would YOU Like to Build a Comission Free Sales Force that Referred You Business and Get You Massive Results for Your Bottom Line?

You can use the same system that we use to build relationships with our clients and keep them giving repeat business and quality referrals! This system will allow you to...

- Log onto your database via any internet connection 24/7!
- Send a customized greeting card (these get opened unlike regular junk mail, which gets throw in the trash!)
- Notify you of the most important dates such as birthdays, anniversaries, etc!
- Allow you to group your contacts!
- And you can do all of this for less than $1.50 per card including the stamp!

NO MORE LICKING, WRITING, OR STAMPING & YOUR MAIL IS GURANTEED TO BE OPENED EVERYTIME!

Find out more today at
www.sendoutcards.com/78840

SPECIAL BONUS! get our exclusive client concierge form and Report on 99 ways to grow your business when you sign up!

SendOutCards™
'Changing Lives... One Card at a Time'

Go to www.sendoutcards.com/79525
And see how you can get started today!!

Are You Looking for a Fun, Entertaining and Educational Speaker?
• Sales Seminars • Conferences • Trade Shows
• Church Conferences • Chambers • Colleges
www.themarketingevangelist.com/speaker

Attn Small Business Owners and Entrepreneurs:

Have you been praying for an answer to your sales, marketing, and motivational problems? If so then, the answer has arrived.....

Every week, Tim and Nick bring you a new sales, marketing, or motivational sermon to help you grow your business!

And best of all, they are free!! All you need to do is visit www.themarketingevangelist.com/podcast to listen online or subscribe for free in I-tunes!

Be sure to check them out today, you will be glad you did!

Thank You for purchasing our book!
Get Our FREE Sales Growth Kit!

We know that sales can be tough without the right tools.

As our way of saying thank you, we have put together a special page on our website where you can get some really cool and valuable business building tools for FREE!!

Just go to

www.themarketingevangelist.com/dude

You will get our complete library of
Sales goals worksheets
Daily Time worksheets
Goal Setting worksheets
Plus much more!!!

www.ingramcontent.com/pod-product-compliance
Lightning Source LLC
Chambersburg PA
CBHW020451220526
45464CB00002B/950